smartlittleowl.com

GW01451489

MY FIRST FOOTBALL COLOURING BOOK

THIS BOOK BELONGS TO:

- -

- -

Receive a FREE gift!

Go to our website and download for free the printable tracing book.

smartlittleowl.com/gift

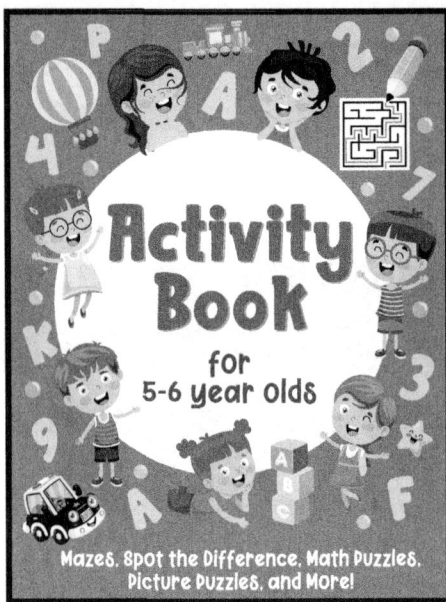

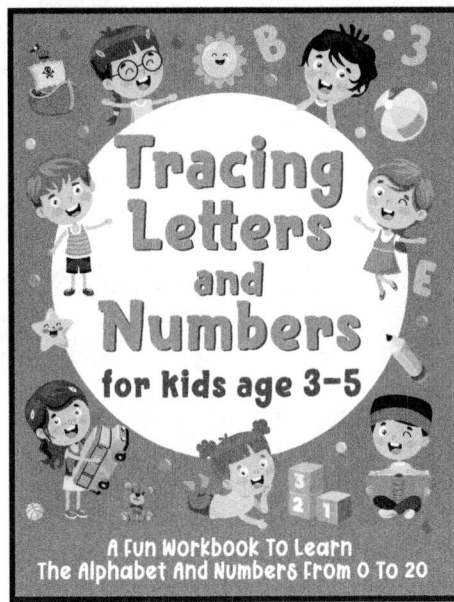

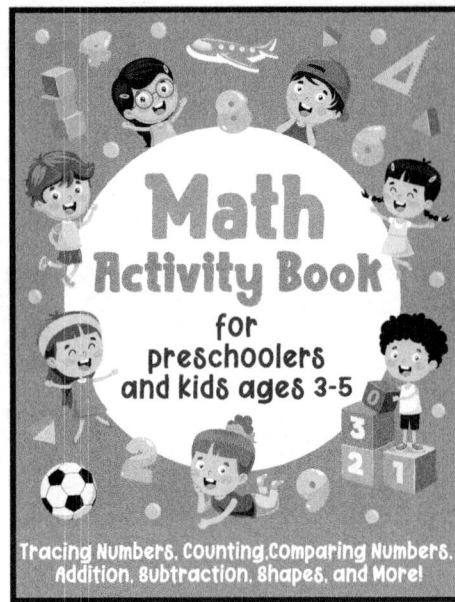

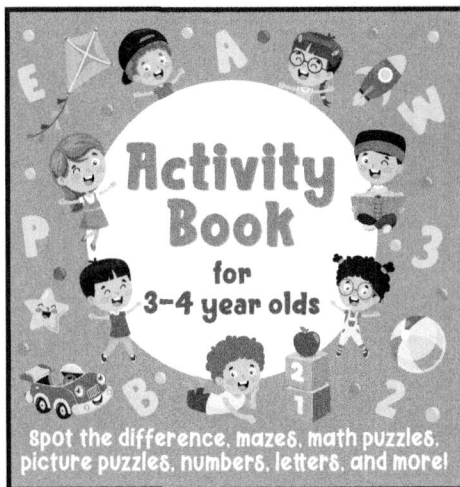

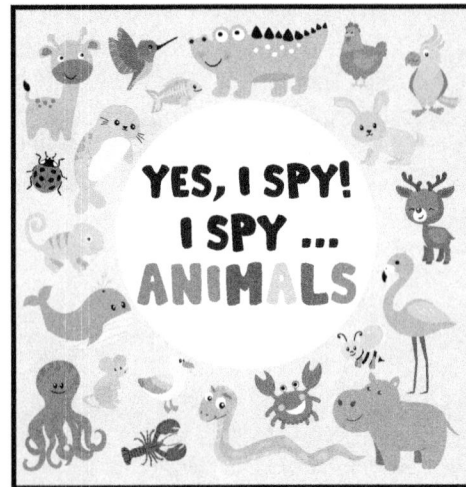

SEE MORE OF OUR PRODUCTS

amazon

Books ▾ | smart little owl | 🔍

Printed in Great Britain
by Amazon